Tattooing is an age-old form of body modification that involves permanently embedding ink in skin to create designs or images. **Tattoo artists** are professionals who design and apply tattoos to all areas of customers' bodies with specialized needles. When dealing with customers, tact and patience may be required. Long periods of sitting are often a part of the job, as some designs take a considerable amount of time to create. Evening and weekend work is usually necessary as well. According to payscale.com, tattoo artists earned a median annual salary of $30,671 as of January 2016.

Compile a Portfolio

Aspiring tattoo artists should possess great artistic ability and creativity. Before an artist can gain an apprenticeship working in a shop, he or she needs to complete a **professional portfolio** exhibiting his or her best works of art. The portfolio should showcase the artist's versatility and ability to draw a variety of subjects. A portfolio can contain both original works and high-quality photographs of drawings.

Taking art classes, either in high school or through a local community center, can help an aspiring tattoo artist learn various art skills, including scale, proportion and shading, all of which are necessary to work successfully as a tattoo artist.

Complete an Apprenticeship

The **Alliance of Professional Tattooists**, or APT for short, recommends an apprenticeship of at least three years. During an apprenticeship, a prospective artist will work in a shop alongside a professional tattooist learning to design tattoos, to operate a tattoo machine, and sterilize equipment. Additionally, some apprenticeships include lessons on business aspects of tattooing and may prepare aspiring artists to have their own shop. According to the APT, free apprenticeships are rare. An apprentice often pays the artist to teach him or her or signs a contract agreeing to work for the shop he or she apprentices in for a set number of years after the apprenticeship is complete.

Take Tattoo Artist Education Courses

Many skills needed for a successful career as a tattoo artist can be learned from an apprenticeship with a knowledgeable artist, but some health departments and other state and local regulatory agencies also require classroom experience. Seminars in disease prevention and skin diseases and infections and training in blood-borne pathogen prevention may be required for licensing.

Get a License

Most states require licensure for tattoo artists; however, requirements vary by state. Oregon, for example, requires licensees to complete a minimum of 360 hours of training under an approved artist as well as 50 tattoos. A written exam and a skills assessment also are typically necessary for licensing.

Some states require tattoo artists to complete a specified number of continuing education credits to renew their license. Continuing education options are available in the form of seminars and classes.

Joining a professional organization, such as the APT or the Association of Professional Tattoo Artists, can provide a tattoo artist with a variety of continuing education options as well as networking opportunities in the industry. Some organizations, for example, provide services that link potential customers to tattoo artists' online portfolios and hold contests where artists can hone their skills.

From an early age I was always fascinated by tattoos. My father had a couple things hear and there and I would see a heavily tattooed person at the beach or swimming pool was to have an encounter with something exotic. At that time the internet was just getting very popular with social media, there was a couple tattoo TV shows and very little literature on the subject. I remember sending off for a magazine called <u>Body Art</u> or inked magazine. It was impressive stuff, and my tattoo education began there.

<u>Tattooing</u> was exciting then, back in the late 90s. Stepping through the door of a tattoo studio was a rite of passage in itself. My first tattoo was a small Cross I got when I was 16 at an old shop on Fort Myers beach, which was applied to my left upper arm.

As I got more involved in the scene, and more heavily tattooed, windows into this secret world would open – and eventually doors. I became good friends with a few tattoo artists and having seen the work I had designed for myself, my friends encouraged me to start tattooing; I followed their advice and it became my dream. And now my JOB

For many people, now more than ever, tattooing is a dream job, and I understand why. Tattooists can dress any way they want. Once they have the contacts and skills they can work almost anywhere in the world. The job is creative. Tattooists enjoy high social status in their area, whether they are a small town high-street tattooist in provincial Britain, or a hip Insta-famous artist working in Hackney or Kreuzberg. It pays well.

All of the above is true. But so is the fact that tattooing full time will give you a bad back, neck and shoulder problems and damaged wrists. Tattooists also spend hours in intimate contact with people who have questionable hygiene. I once had a memorable few hours tattooing the lower back of a person with a very pungent intergluteal cleft, not to mention the cases of halitosis and athlete's foot I've got up close and personal with over the years.

Customers can be rude to the point of violence. I have been threatened physically after refusing to tattoo someone's face, twice, by the intoxicated. If clients aren't rude, they can be stupid beyond belief. I once had to explain to a young woman in her 20s that getting her boyfriend of two weeks' name tattooed on her crotch was not a good idea. A colleague of mine did the tattoo for her after she pointed out, correctly, that if we didn't do it someone else would. The relationship didn't last – she came back to have it covered a few months later.

While it's true that a hardworking tattooist can earn a decent living, I imagine most clients and potential tattooists have little understanding of how the money side of things works. Ordinarily, a tattooist takes a fee for his work and a percentage (usually 40%-50%) goes to the studio. Tax, holiday and sick pay will come out of the remaining 60%. Taking into account the time spent preparing the design, and the (often unpaid) time spent as an apprentice gives a more realistic view of tattooists' earnings. As we are paid on a commission basis, a good day can bring in £500, a bad day nothing. Of course, most days fall somewhere in between.

The creative side of tattooing is often overstated as well. Many artists will find themselves doing the same trite cliches and sentimental claptrap day in and day out. Personally, I hate anything without imagination or mystery, such as tattoos related to football, patriotism, song lyrics and names. I will turn them down and lose money rather than do them.

There are many talented artists pushing boundaries and taking the art form in new and exciting directions, but this is generally limited to a few studios operating out of more culturally dynamic places, and does not represent the reality of working in one of the hundreds of studios across the UK. Tattooing in Britain has taken its place on the high street, alongside hair dye and acrylic nails, to become just another part of the narcissistic, selfie-obsessed culture of the 21st century.

The biggest change, and for me the worst, that I have seen in tattooing has been its acceptance by mainstream society. Tattooing has lost its outsider status. Tattooed people are no longer seen as mad, bad and dangerous to know. A new tattoo means little more than a few likes on Instagram. It has all the danger of a Sex Pistols T-shirt hanging in a Topshop window. Like that other stalwart of rebellion, rock and roll, body art has been commodified to the point of irrelevance.

The job is something I'm grateful to do, but feel increasingly trapped in. I am currently working on a novel, not the most reliable choice of career to try and break in to, but one that allows similar levels of personal freedom.

Tattooing is like an ugly, misunderstood and unnerving creature living on the ocean floor, for years the stuff of legend and rumour. Drag this brittle and malformed freak of nature to the surface and it crumbles and dies; better it had been left in the depths.

Learning to tattoo is a labor of love. Even if you're an exceptional artist on canvas, that doesn't mean you'll start off tattooing like you were born with a <u>tattoo machine</u> in hand. You'll need to spend at least a year doing an apprenticeship, and **not in your house** "get certified" in first aid and OSHA's Blood borne Pathogen Standard, get a license (if required in your state), and practice, practice, practice! And that's just a down-and-dirty overview of what it takes to become a tattoo artist.

If you think you want to be a tattoo artist, go to shops and talk to all your local artist…Piercing and tattoo artists are your bread and butter we're always happy to see fresh new talent on the scene. We just want you to know what's involved before you take the plunge, so that you can make an informed decision about choosing this career path--a path that more and more artists are choosing as tattoos become progressively more mainstream and demand for great ink continues to rise.

So what is involved in becoming a tattoo artist? Is it enough to be a good artist on canvas, or does tattooing require a different level of artistic talent? Is it a skill you can develop or something you're either born to do or not? Is an apprenticeship absolutely required? How do you find a reputable shop to employ you when you're ready? We may not have the answer to every question about becoming a tattoo artist that's bouncing around your brain, but we can tell you enough to help you make an informed decision as to whether or not tattooing the profession for you.

How to Become a Tattoo Artist

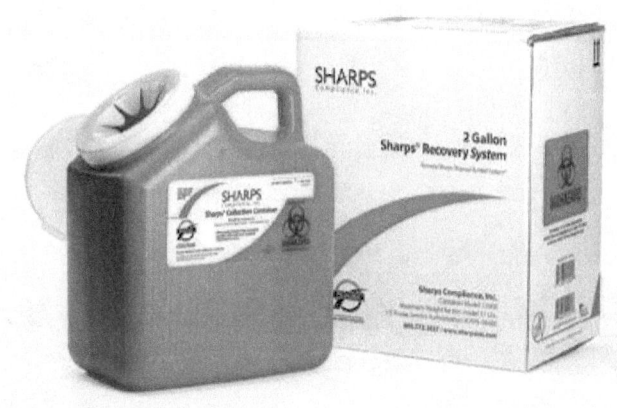

101

Study Art. To be a successful tattoo artist, you need to have an innate ability to create art. You don't have to be Picasso, but you need to be able to draw fairly well. Being able to paint or create art in other mediums is a plus, but not required. A knack for the craft of creating art isn't enough, though; as with other trades, tattooing requires specialized training. Some of that training can be done at a traditional college or art school, since basic art classes are a great foundation for learning the art of tattooing. What kind of art classes should you consider taking? Drawing, portraiture and even calligraphy classes will all give you some essential building blocks for inking great tattoos later on.

Get Basic Medical Training. It's also important to learn about first aid, blood borne pathogens, and lab safety. You'll need your first aid certification so you can handle yourself and the situation if an issue arises with a client--say, if someone passes out or starts having an allergic reaction to <u>skin prep</u>, <u>tattoo ink</u> or even your gloves. (Latex allergies are all too common these days, which is why we offer <u>nitrile gloves</u>, too.)

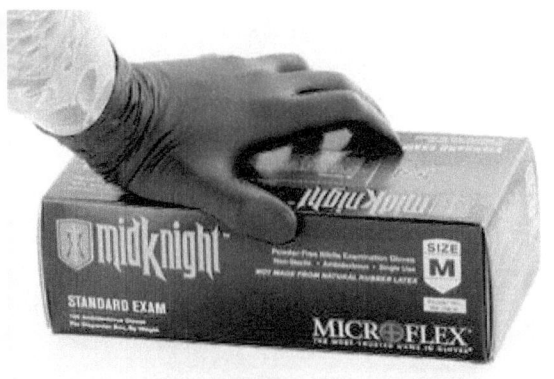

OSHA requires that all tattoo and piercing shop employees have their <u>bloodborne pathogens certification</u>, and it's good for you because it will teach you how to avoid incidents like nasty accidental needle sticks. Lab safety may seem like the odd man out, but think about the clean room at the heart of a tattoo and piercing shop; it's essentially a lab! Learning about <u>sterilization methods</u> and how to safely maneuver around a lab setting will only make your life as a tattoo artist easier. Plus it'll help protect your and your clients' health and hopefully prevent you from running into the legal issues that can arise from not maintaining a sterile work environment. (See our *Tattooing Safely: A Guide for Tattoo Artists* article for more on this subject.)

Do a Tattoo Apprenticeship. never ever ever Tattoo out of your home Next up, find a tattoo apprenticeship. There are tattoo artists who get around this step and still become successful, but hands-on training with a mentor is truly the best way to learn this craft. You may have to comb shops well beyond your area--possibly even go to another state--to find one that wil take you on as an apprentice, but it'll be worth your effort. You can pull together a list of shops where you might like to do an apprenticeship and/or specific artists who you'd be honored to have mentor you using the internet. Then, start making calls, or better yet, hit the pavement. You may have to return to a shop repeatedly before they'll consider letting you apprentice there, but if you feel strongly about having a specific artist or team of artists train you, don't

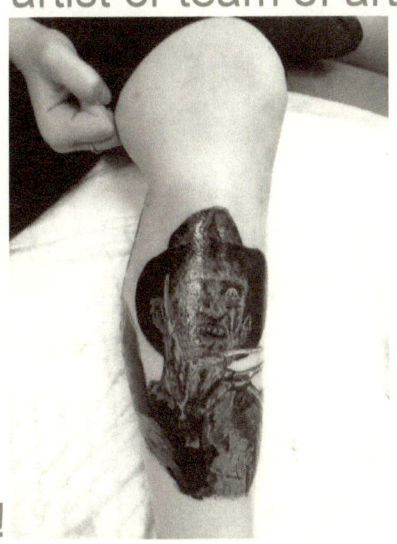

give up!

 Tattoo Afterlife . I myself have brrn turned away repeatedly, but I didn't give up. I would go home and practice on pig skin and other things never another human, and then practice some more, often working from 5 a.m. until late at night to perfect his skills until he finally put together a portfolio that made once of the shops pause. His raw talent was amazing, particularly since I was just a *kid* as far as the shop was concerned. So I gotan apprentice, and now I was one of the hottest young tattoo artists on the scene--all because of my perseverance and hard work. If there's an artist you're that passionate about working with, show them why you're worth their time, and maybe you'll be the, who was a tattoo prodigy before the age of 20!

Practice, Practice, Practice! There's nothing like experience to make you an experienced tattoo artist. At first, you should use <u>practice skin</u> or even fruit to practice. (Oranges work best if you go the fruit route.) Next, you might upgrade to tattooing yourself. Eventually you'll be able to work on real clients, under your Master's supervision and with the clients' consent, of course. (It's amazing how many willing, paying customers will take advantage of a lower rate even at the cost of a newbie permanently marring their skin!) The more practice you get, the better your tattooing skills will become, and the more great pieces you'll have done that you can show off in your portfolio.

Find a Job. After a year-long apprenticeship, which likely paid, you'll need to find a job and start making some money. How much can you expect to earn? It's hard to say, since there are a lot of variables that impact average salaries. Location, economic conditions, and your talent level are just a few of those factors. That said, the average U.S.-based tattoo artist makes anywhere from $30,000 to $45,000 annually according to **Indeed.com** (varies by region, with Northern California being one of the higher pay range areas). When you get started, you aren't likely to hit the average, but it isn't impossible. Striking out on your own could eventually allow you to make more money, but when you're first getting started, it's usually better to go to work in a shop.

Sometimes shops will ask their apprentices to stay on and become resident artists after they finish their studies. That isn't always the case, though, so be prepared to start looking for a job in another shop as you wrap up your apprenticeship. Your Master may have some suggestions for you or pair you up with friends at another shop, or you may have to hit the pavement again. Make sure you take a portfolio with you when you go. Business cards and a letter of recommendation from your Master are also good assets to have handy when you're looking for a new tattoo shop to call home.

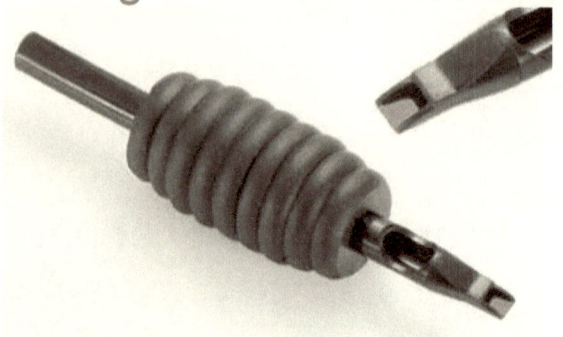

Build Your Reputation. Great tattoo artists who aren't constantly letting the world know how great they are are poor tattoo artists. You have to actively work on building your reputation if you want to make a living tattooing. The internet is your best tool for brand building. Get on Facebook, Instagram and any other social media site you can keep up with regularly, post photos of your work, make announcements about special events where you'll be, share tips like tattoo aftercare-- anything you can think of to engage people. Create an online portfolio in our <u>Gallery</u>, and share a link to it on your business cards and social media profiles. Sign up for listings on tattoo directory sites. Attend conventions. Make glossy, full-color flyers that feature your work and pass them out to anyone who will take them. Get creative! There are *so* many ways you can promote yourself. As long as you pursue a few of them *and* you're a decent tattoo artist, your client base should grow steadily over time.

Sanitation and the Law

Tattoo parlors and artists are mandated by law to adhere to regulations for their own good and their clients. A lot of people are already aware of these regulations, and for good reasons they tend to choose compliant parlors rather than non-compliant parlors. Therefore, sticking to guidelines really helps tattoo parlors retain customers and stay in business.

All tattoo parlors must adhere to rules set by the Occupational Safety and Health Administration (OSHA) and Centers for Disease Control & Prevention (CDC). Tattoo parlors are subject to such regulations simply because the nature of their work literally involves shedding blood. Blood and many other body fluids are vectors of pathogens, notably ones that cause serious debilitating illnesses such as hepatitis B and C, and acquired immune deficiency syndrome (AIDS). This is the reason why there are stringent rules for tattoo parlors.

The main goal of these regulations is to prevent and reduce blood exposure generated during tattooing. Actually, these regulations are fairly easy to follow. Here are most important bits of these regulations.

Universal rules

Tattoo parlors and tattoo artists must observe universal precautions to all clients. During work, the tattoo artist must wear barrier gowns, gloves, goggles or eyeglasses and face shield to avoid contact and exchange of body fluids. The gloves and barrier gowns, in particular, must be changed after each client.

All implements that will be in contact with the client's skin and blood must be of single-use, or can be completely sterilized.

All materials applied to skin of clients must be from bulk, commercially-packaged, single-use containers only. This applies to dyes or pigments used in tattooing. It must be stored in an area away from toilets or other areas with high-contamination levels.

Make sure to employ barrier protection whenever handling hazardous and sharps waste.

Floor plan requirements and rules for furnishings

There must be a separate work area and waiting area for the customers. The tattoo work area must be constructed to allow privacy to clients. The whole studio must be well-ventilated and have adequate lighting. The tattoo parlor must have a clean and working toilet and a utility sink.

The work area must have a clean sink and basin, with running cold and hot water.

The body art studio must be constructed in a manner that allows easy cleaning. For example, walls and ceilings must be light in color and the floors must not be carpeted (because it absorbs blood).

The furnishings in the tattoo parlor must be made of nonabsorbent, corrosive resistant and smooth material that is easily sanitized. This applies to work tables, countertops and chairs.

Each artist must have his or her own work tables, chairs and own set of cabinets for instruments, dyes and single-use articles.

Guidelines for sterilization and sanitation

Non-disposable devices and instruments must be first scrubbed in hot water and soap, and then sterilized in an autoclave.

Acetate stencils, if used, must be sterilized using an antibacterial solution after each use.

Paper stencils are for single-use only, and must be disposed in the hazardous bin after each use.

Markers used to draw designs onto the client's skin must be single-use only.

A new and sterile tattoo needle must be used in each client. For safety, use forceps to attach and remove tattoo needle into the machine. Never manipulate the needle, clean or used, by hand.

Clean and single-use gloves must be readily available at the workplace. Gloves must be changed with each client, and when it's punctured or cut. Used gloves must be thrown away in the hazardous waste bin.

The work tables and chairs must be sanitized with a bactericidal solution after each client.

Guidelines during and after tattoo procedure

Tattoo artists with diarrhea, vomiting, fever or rash or skin infections are not allowed to perform tattooing procedure.

Before starting the tattooing procedure, the tattoo artists must first inspect his or her hands for hangnails, cuts and sores. All cuts and sores must be bandaged, and fingernails trimmed, before tattooing.

All pieces of jewelry including watches and rings must be removed before tattooing.

Before the tattooing procedure, the tattoo artist must first wash his or her hands with warm water and antibacterial soap using a hand brush. Then, dry the hands using a blow drier.

The tattoo artist must first don intact disposable latex, or nitrile gloves and an apron, or smock. The tattoo artist must change or dispose of these after each use or when torn or punctured.

The needles and tattoo machine tubes must be of single-use only. Use new set of needles and tattoo machine tubes for each client, and after tattooing, they must be disposed in the sharps waste bin.

Only use single-use razors to shave the skin area, and they must be changed for each client. After use, these razors must be disposed in the sharps waste bin.

Tattoo artists may not smoke or eat in the body art studio.

Guidelines for waste disposal

All wipes and bandages must be disposed in the hazardous waste bin.

After the tattoo has been applied, the area must be washed with a single-use towel soaked in an antibacterial solution. Discard this towel into the hazardous waste bin.

Used gloves, ointment applicator, wipes and drapes must be disposed in the hazardous waste bin.

Bandages, wipes and exclusion drapes (if used) must be of single-use only and must be changed for each client. Used and bloody bandages, wipes and exclusion drapes must be disposed in the conspicuously-marked hazardous waste bin.

About waste bins in tattoo parlors

A separate bin for hazardous waste must be located at the workplace of the tattoo parlor. Do not dispose household waste in this bin.

Another separate bin exclusive for sharps must be located at the workplace of the tattoo parlor. The bin for sharps must be solidly built, has puncture-resistant and leakproof walls, and must have narrow mouth and sealable. The sharps bin must be conspicuously marked.

There must be a separate waste bin for household waste in the waiting area and work area. Never put hazardous waste and sharps waste in this waste bin.

Hazardous and sharps waste must be collected and disposed by a licensed contractor. Disposing waste contaminated with blood and sharps as household waste could land you in trouble. Save yourself from the trouble by having waste generated by tattoo parlors, specifically the hazardous waste and sharps, be disposed by a licensed medical waste disposal provider to make sure state and federal guidelines are followed.

Needles

Needles should be disposed of after each tattoo into a biohazard "sharps" container. Only new needles should ever be used. You should be able to witness your artist taking the needles out of their original packs when he's setting up for your new ink. If he doesn't have anything to hide, he'll let you watch.

Single Use Markers and Stencils

Unless your artist is free-handing the design, he will use either a transfer paper or markers to draw the design onto your skin. Generally, you will approve the positioning of it from this phase of the process. Make sure that the markers and transfer paper being used is single-use… as in disposable. Don't let someone draw on you with a Sharpie that he just used to draw on a previous customer or worse yet, his boots. It's a Universal Precaution that is often overlooked.

Gloves and Hand Washing

Obviously your artist should wear gloves when he tattoos you. Watch him though. Make sure he's washing his hands thoroughly with an antibacterial soap prior to putting new gloves on. Make sure he uses paper towel to shut off the water, not the hands he just got clean. If you're allergic to latex, let them know so they can wear another type of glove. Here at The Shop, we don't even use the latex kind because we don't want to risk the allergies.

Ink

The general rule is, if there's ink on it, there's blood on it. The area should not have any ink stains anywhere. All ink should be placed ink caps on his work tray for the tattooing process before it begins. Once the process has begun, he shouldn't grab the bottle of ink for a refill without removing his gloves, washing his hands first and then rewashing and re-gloving before touching you again.

The Machine's Cord

If there's a chance the artist's tattoo machine cord will touch your body, make sure they use a cover. Imagine a cord without a cover sliding up against someone else's skin, then the ground, then your skin. That's just disgusting.

Paper Towel

Paper towel is needed to wipe as you go during the tattoo process, however, observe how your artist grabs it. Usually we will set up plenty of fresh paper towel at the station for ease of use. What if that runs out though? Paper towel should be on a dispenser so that his hands never touch the rest of the roll or the inside of the role. If you see this happen, he should just go ahead and throw that roll away, and rewash and re-glove.

Cross Contamination

Every tattoo artist when cleaning up his area should have what he considers a dirty hand and a clean hand. The artist should not use the hand he was rinsing tubes with to open a drawer, regardless of the status of his gloves. He should be using only his clean hand to touch surfaces that are considered "clean."

Ultrasonic Cleaner

When the tubes are taken off the machine, they are deposited into a bleach sanitation tub while they await the next step, which is to be placed in an ultrasonic cleaner. The shop has to have one of these. It prepares the tubes for the autoclave. It sends a super speed sound waves through the metal and it breaks down contaminants. It doesn't however provide adequate sterilization. For that, you need an autoclave.

Autoclave

Your artist will have a functioning autoclave that is regularly spore tested that he will clean his tubes and such in. (At the Shop, we send out our spore tests once a month.) These get placed in little baggies. On the baggies, there will be a little area built into it that shows if it's been through a sterilization process. Ask to see it if you have any concerns. This goes the same for piercings. Ask to see the baggy. Scratchers will tell you that they boil the stuff in bleach or something along those lines. Well, that's not good enough. It simply won't keep all bloodborne pathogens off the equipment.

Bathrooms

Before your tattoo, ask to use the bathroom. Just like at restaurants, the cleanliness of a shops bathroom is a good indicator of the cleanliness of the shop's artists.

Go ahead and ask your artist about their sterilization procedures, make sure he knows and follows them. If he gives you crap or doesn't know the basics, just turn around, walk out the door and come see me for your new tattoo.

Tattoo machine Basics

Set up tattoo machine is an importanmt procedure for users to tattoo, and there is some instructions for you to set up your tattoo machine:

1 First you should assemble machine and the first step is to set barrel, please look at the tattoo grip a tube inside it ,on the two sides of the grip there are two screw, the screws is to fix the tube and tattoo tip, you could slap the tube at preferable length inside the grip and fix it by adjust tool like this.

Then fix the tips also at your favorable lenghth, fix it just as the tube.

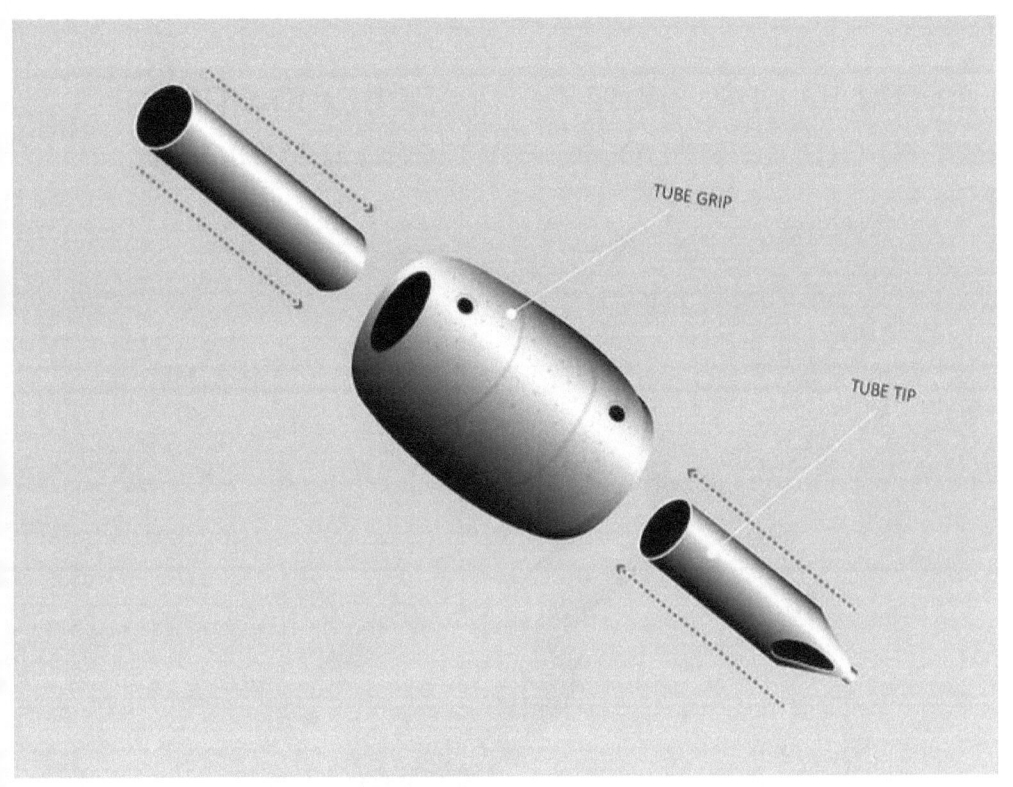

2 The second step is set up needles ,now you can see from the back of its package, it says RL RS M1 M2 RM or F, this tell the size of needles
We take one out, and begin to assemble it . two tips when set up needle,
One is please make sure the projection downward.
Second you should not bump the top of

needle to any place of the tips and grip so not to dull the needle and lead to painful tattoo.

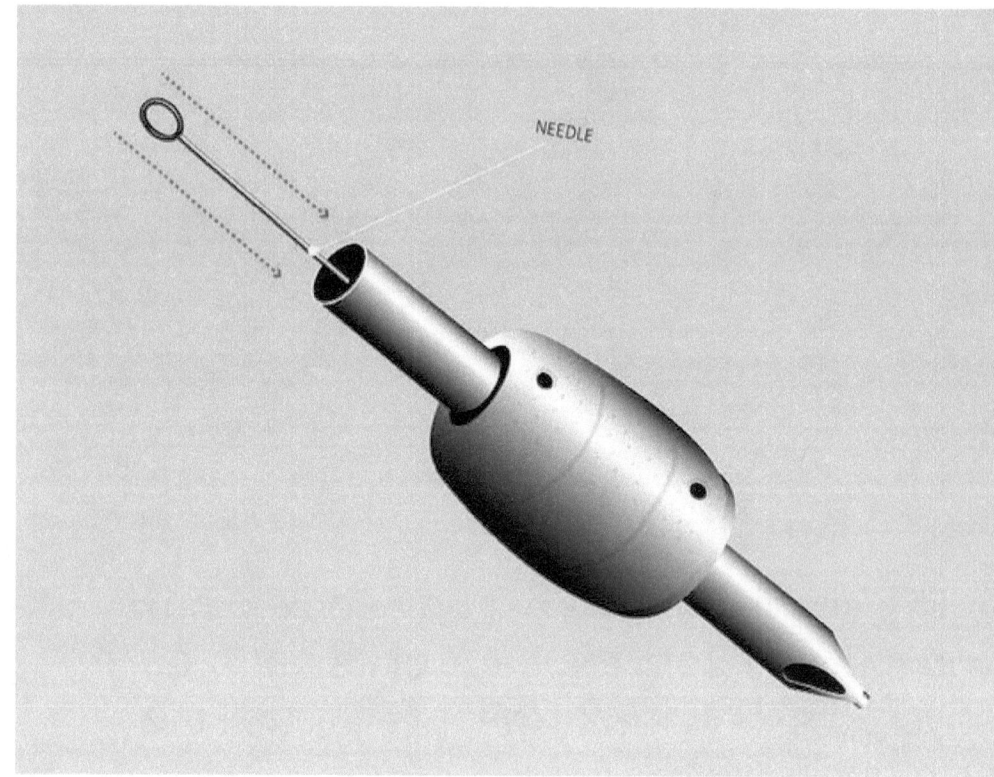

3 Put a nipple on the armature bar pin. That is where the top of your needle will be connected around. Slap the needles and attach it to the nipple.

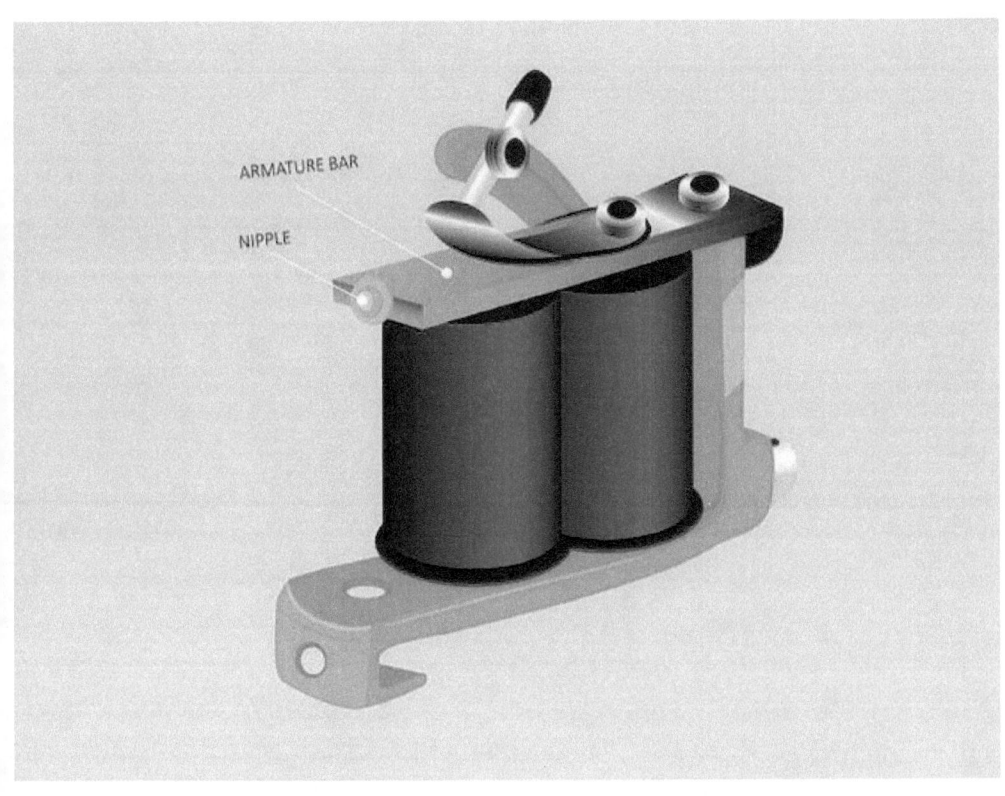

4 Hang needles on the gromments.

After grip is assmebled ok ,we need to adjust the length of needles it comes out. What we can see for this needles is around 1mm to 1.5 mm.When grip and needles are adjust well ,we can screw up the grip.

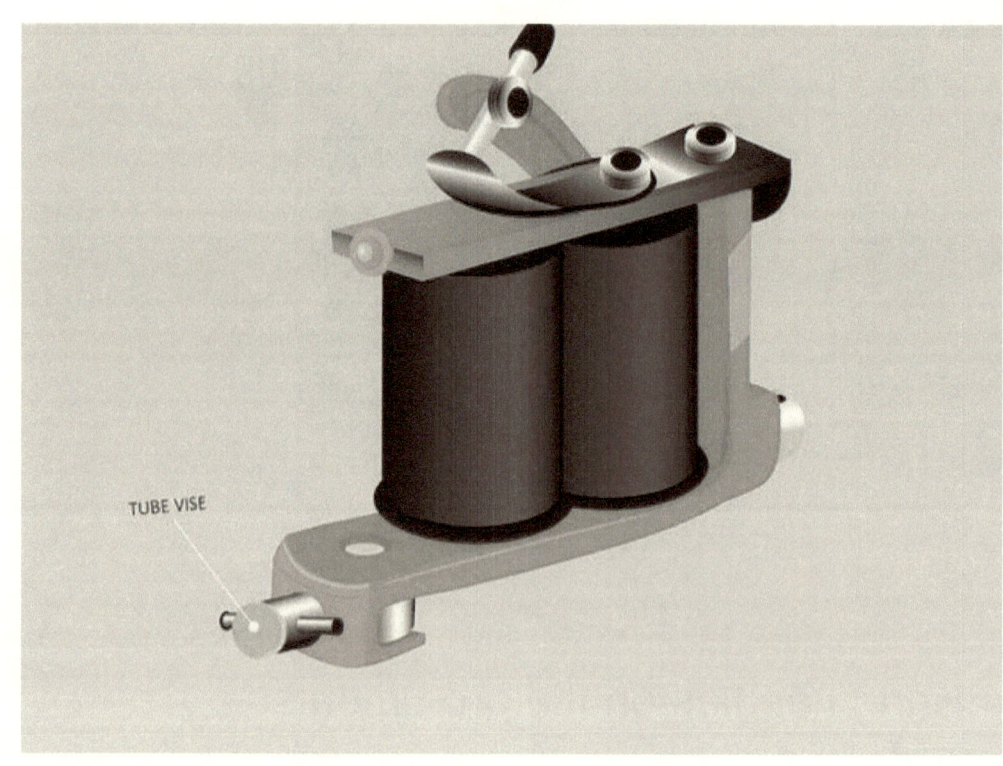

5 This is the whole step of how to assmeble tattoo machine.

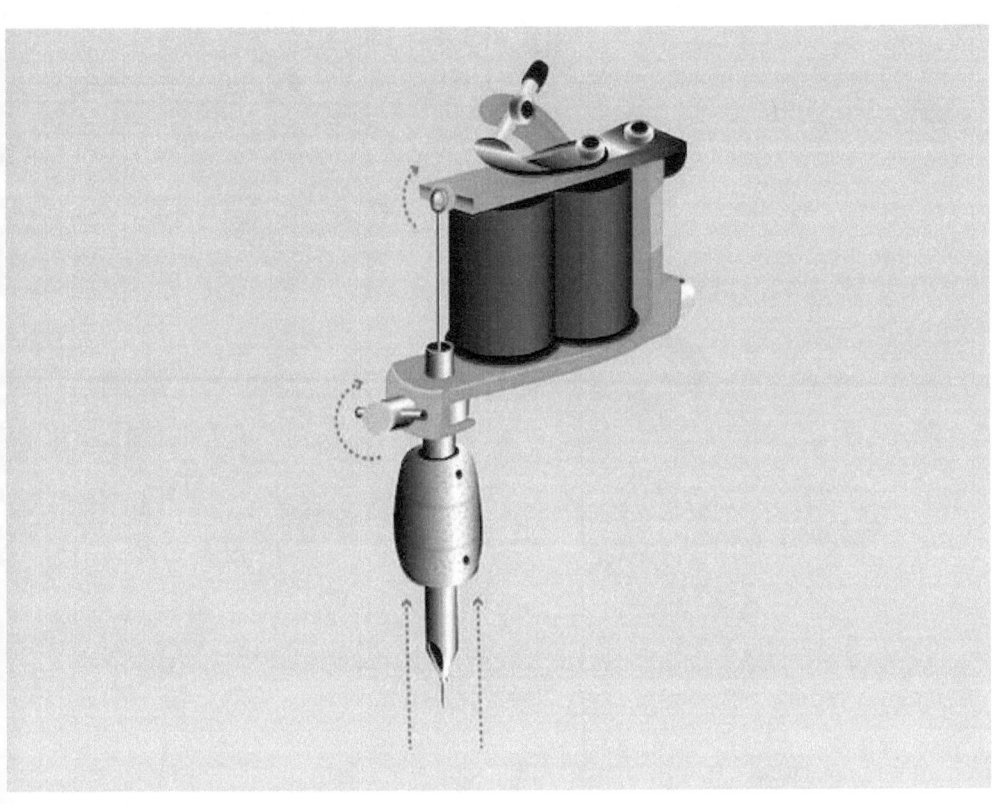

6 Connect the foot pedal, clip cord and power pack to the gun.

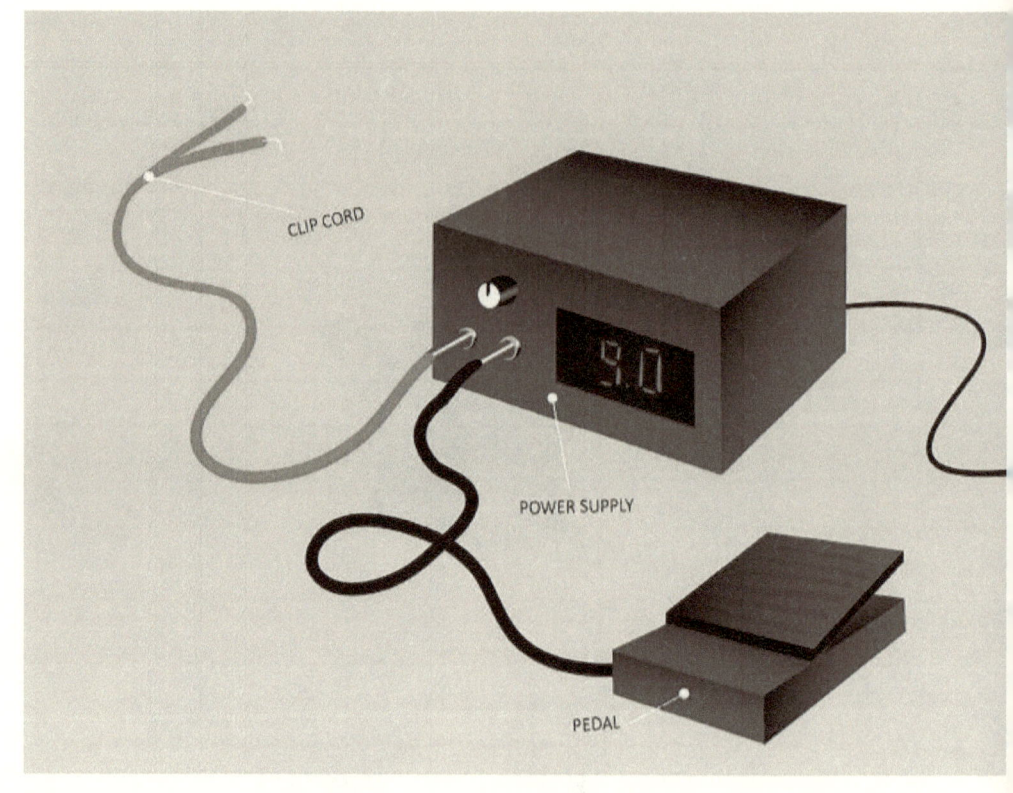

Machine Tuning

Machine tuning is hands down the most important thing you will need to know about machines themselves. I can't tell you how many times I have heard someone say, "I don't need to know how to tune a machine. I just use it out of the box and its fine." This kills me. If you are going to operate any kind of tool you need to know how to do so properly. The theory behind tuning your machine is to get the machine running as smooth as possible. The less vibration the easier operation will be. If you want a smooth straight line then the machine has to be in tune. When tuning a machine, many factors come into play. Your grommet on the armature nipple needs to be in good shape and your o ring on the front spring also needs to be in good condition. Another thing not everyone looks at is the quality of the contact screw. If it's dirty or has carbon build-up it will not get a nice smooth connection. Contact screws can be made from brass, steel, copper, and silver. Copper is fair, stainless and brass will work, but in my personal opinion silver is the better choice. Brass and steel are a very hard metal and they also spark a little. Over time they will burn a hole all the way through the tip of a front spring. If the machine is out of tune it will burn a hole much faster. Silver is a softer metal so front springs will last a very long time. Silver is also less incline to spark so you have less problems with plastic machine covers. The only thing I don't like about silver and brass is that they tarnish. Because silver is a very soft metal you have to be careful not to tighten you're set screw to hard, it can eat the threads right off of the contact screw.

You also want to take a look at the hole in the frame that your front binding post screws into. Almost all machines have a longer hole than needed. The reason for this is more adjustment. With the machine sitting on its yoke, if you barely loosen the screw you can move the entire front binding post assembly up or down to adjust for lining or shading. Moving the front binding post upward is better for color and shading, down is better for lining, and the center is universal. I just run the binding post in the center. Either way you set this option, the tip of your contact screw should be dead center in line with the hole for your tube vice. The best way to check the alignment is to hold the machine like a pistol that you're about to fire. Hold the machine so that you can see the contact screw tip closer to you. While holding the machine at this angle, move your head a little to one side to see if the machine is level. If not pivot the "contact screw" up or down till it is level. You can check to see if the armature bar is also in the center position by doing the same thing only looking in the tube hole with the armature bar away from you. The more in line the armature bar and the tip of the contact screw are to the center of the machine then the less resistance you have while the needle bar is in motion. This will make for a steadier stroke.

I have already talked a little about the stroke but what exactly is it? The stroke of your machine is the distance traveled by your armature bar while in motion. The duty cycle of the machine is the length of time that the front spring stays in contact with the contact screw. The duty cycle is measured in percentages. If your duty cycle is 50% then the time the front spring touches the contact screw and time it does not touch the contact screw while open is the same. If the duty cycle of the machine is 40% then the front spring is in contact with the contact screw 40% of the time and away from the contact screw 60% of the time. Studies have shown that optimum duty cycle is around 55%. This can be measured by using an electronic multimeter that has a duty cycle setting on it. You attach one lead to the clip cord post in the spring saddle and the other lead to the contact screw. Some newer power supplies come equipped with a duty cycle reader. The stroke strength is hand measured by taking your thumb while the machine is off and pressing on the armature bar nipple. You want to push the armature bar all the way to the coils. If you apply pressure to the front spring then it will bend and you will not get an accurate measurement. The old way of machine tuning is a little less technical. If you've been around tattooing you may have hear of the old nickel and dime trick. A nickel is about two millimeters thick and a dime is about one and a half millimeters thick. The nickel and dime trick means that if you can just fit a nickel in that space then you're good for lining, and a dime if good for shading. This is not always the case.

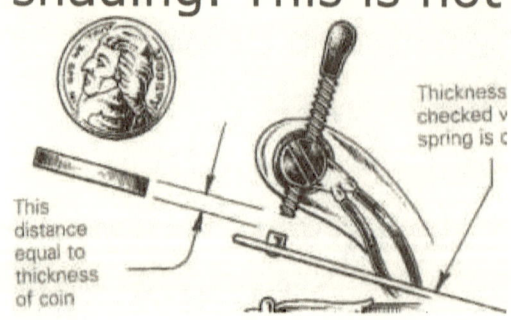

Thickness should be checked when spring is depressed

CONTACT POINT

The idea is that if your lining, then you need to be a little deeper so you're black is darker, while shading your working the skin a little more so you don't want as much depth to avoid scarring. Definitely sounds like a good idea, but all this does it set the stroke a little different and it does not smooth out the action of the machine. Like a few close held ideas about tattooing, this was cool for the sixties but not by today's standards.

Most tattoo artist use two machines in the course of one tattoo. You set one machine up for shading and one for lining. Doing this means you don't have to switch needles and tubes. You just use one for each. Since this is a guide for beginners, most apprentices can only afford one machine at first (speaking as a veteran artist I find it's easier to do this anyway) you can also set one machine up universally to do both. I set a few machines up to do different things and different styles but any artist can tell you they have one machine that they like more than any other.

To set a machine up for lining you want to adjust the front binding post all the way down, as far from the top of the frame arm as possible. Make sure to pivot the contact screw tip to the dead center of the tube vice; unless you choose to use a cutback. For a liner, if the machine is sitting on the yoke and you are looking at the frame side, the contact screw will be at about six o'clock, where a shader will be about four o'clock. Some machines are made specifically to accommodate these angles, and some are universal. If your front spring isn't touching the contact screw just right then loosen it and move it up till it fully touches the screw tip. To properly tune your machine

Coloring a tattoo basics

The process of coloring a tattoo is a relatively simple if you always remember and apply a few key rules and regularly practice them The technique is the same for solid black tattooing as it is for solid coloring. Actually, black is a little easier as black ink seems more readily accepted by the skin than colored ink The motion is a circular one, and coloring a tattoo is done in small circular steps. If constant pace is maintained, a lot of area can be covered in a small amount of time. Each circle just barely overlapping the last circle until the areas are covered solid in just two sweeps. Never do an area more than once or twice over Just small constant, flowing circles covers an area smooth and efficiently, and always working off the tips of the needles,

Don t press hard and don't stay in one area repeatedly crossing or try to color the skin like with a crayon or pencil. This will turn the skin to hamburger and create a bad scab or possibly, leave scars, the ultimate error. While the needles are in contact With the skin, keep

the machine moving, never hold It still or that will cut the skin Don't go back over. Get it right the first sweep through. It will look better. The more holes the more bleeding the more scabbing, and the more ink will be absorbed out in the scab "Packing it in" won't get you anywhere so let the machine do the job and pay attention to the work being done, A little area is done and then wiped to be inspected. Continue in this fashion and monitor the results. Any adjustments can be quickly made when done in this manner. The color or the tattoo will not be any more colorful or brighter when you try to hammer the color into the skin.

circles

Small tight circles

Small tight

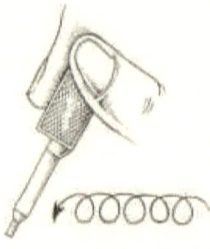

When applying color to a tattoo, puddles of ink will get all over the skin, sometimes totally obscuring the outline. It's not good to be in such a hurry as to not take the time to continually wipe the excess away. Tattoos are ruined by running the color over the outline. By continually wiping away all the excess color, strict attention can be paid to what one is doing and where one is going. When inspecting work in progress, the skin must be stretched tight (as if tattooing) so any mistakes will be readily picked up. If the color is solid when the skin is stretched, it will be solid when relaxed in a normal position.

If the area that is to be a solid color has skin showing through, (it is not solid, but is sketchy looking and has pockets of skin that aren't colored) something must be done to correct this problem. The easiest solution is that the tattooing circles are not small enough. Make littler circles, cover a smaller area and slow down a hit. Another reason is that the needles are not in contact with the skin at all times. This means that in all the tattooing excitement, the machine is not kept steady and the needles are being lifted up off the skin in some areas. This doesn't mean to press harder, but to just keep the needles in the skin. Let the machine sink the needles, you keep the machine in line. Another reason for open pockets in the coloring is that the color itself was not properly mixed. Be sure to shake the bottles of ink good before using. This will maintain an even color value within the bottle. Stick to the small flowing circles, letting the machine take care of the tattooing and good results will be obtained. When you come across tiny areas that can't be done with a shader. use a three or five needle outliner.

For the coloring process, the needle tips should hang out of the tube end just so you can feel them and ought to extend out of the tube around 116 inch when the machine is running. This setting will keep the color flowing in but won't really plow into the skin. Overzealous tattooist can get carried away and this machine setting is extra insurance against scarring and bleeding. Later on in your career, the setting can be changed to a longer stroke, but only when the feel of coloring is totally familiar and confidence is assured that you have everything under control.

Every time a different color or shade is used, the tube and needles of the machine must be thoroughly cleaned. Haphazardly dipping into colors can't bechanced because sloppy and muddy mixes will lie the result. The only way just pure color can be obtained is to have 101) percent clean needles and tubes each time. Clean out the tube between colors by running the machine under hot water until the machine basically washes itself clean. Be sure to run the needles across a tissue in reverse motion to remove all excess water from the tube tip Never do this in a forward motion because it will pick up pieces of paper tissue between the needles. Get in the habit of doing this every time in between color applications and it will ensure good clean color tones. After completing every color on a customer, spray the area with a green soap spray, wash and apply over the area a thin coat of Vaseline. The Vaseline will fill some pores and keep other colors from entering the holes and spoiling the color.

When putting in color, a certain sequence must be followed in order for a tattoo to come out the best possible. If it is not followed, muddy mixtures will appear, clouding up the tattoo and spoiling it with dull tones. The basics for the sequence are simple. Colors must be applied from the darkest tones to the lighter ones. This is why black shading is the first thing done after the outline. All solid black and the black shading is the darkest color and must be applied first. The color sequence after this is as follows: 1) Dark purple. 2) Blues. 3)Greens. 4) Light Purple. 5) Browns. 6) Reds. 7)Orange. 8) Yellow. 9) White.

How To Shade A Tattoo

To learn how to shade a tattoo, you usually have to attend extended classes or training sessions. After all, it's a part of learning how to do a tattoo in the first place. There are a few tricks to shading a tattoo that are lesser known, and several different techniques, so even if you attend training there are certainly techniques that couldn't fit in those sessions. If you are interested in learning or are already an expert looking to learn something new, then these tips on how to shade a tattoo are for you.

The Basics of Tattoo Shading

First up is basic technique. It's common practice to finish the line work before you ever touch it with colors or tattoo shading techniques. This prevents the dark ink of the line work from leeching in to the rest of the colors and making a muddled mess. While some artists opt to dry off the tattoo and wait fifteen minutes before proceeding, it's considered best practice to do the coloring and inking in two entirely different sessions. This also gives the customer some last-minute opportunities to think about the color they want. If they decide to stick to the colors they chose, you know that they know what they want. If they decide to change their mind about the details, thoroughly prod them for the reason why. Both you and they need to be sure that you're doing what they want.

All Black Ink

Once you have all of that sorted out, your technique will differ depending on whether you are making a colored or a black and white tattoo. Let's go over the black and white tattoo, first. As you probably already know, a common shading technique involves just black ink. By dipping the needle in water, you can carefully dilute a solid black pigment into a gray pigment without needing to change needles. When applying the ink, you can tilt the needle and use it in a circular fashion to help blend in the slightly different tones of the ink. By pressing the needle down less deep in lighter areas, you can give the illusion of a fading gradient. If you made a mistake during line work, shading is an easy way to cover it up while making the tattoo look aesthetically pleasing.

From Black To Gray

That might all work well, but if you have the opportunity, try using gray inks instead of diluting black ink. The result is a more permanent shadow that stays on the skin for almost as long as the lines themselves. Plus, it's easier to get a solid gray through this technique. If you expect to have very similar gray tones or to use a cell shading technique, then gray ink is the way to go. There are various styles of gray ink—with some leaning towards a blue or a brown tone—so be sure to test the color on different mediums before applying it to skin. Despite not having a hue of its own, gray can be used as a color itself and bring out many different shades that diluted black can't. And, since you're starting with a midtone, you can use all the techniques that you normally would while producing a much more detailed gradient.

Colors Finally

When using colors, thoughts of shading should come first! The darkness and lightness of a color affects how the tattoo turns out. If you use a light color on top of a dark ink, you end up with a muddled mess. Therefore, you need to pick your colors ahead of time and ink them in a very specific order. Start with light, warm colors such as white, yellow, or lime green, then move on to light cool colors, and then move on to darker colors in the same sequence. Dark purple and blue should always be the last colors you use. In between colors, be sure to clean off your needles carefully. If you don't, the inks will mix and ruin the color before it's even placed on the skin

Plan Ahead

From an artistic standpoint, there are a few things you need to keep in mind. First is your light source: you should always have a light source that is the same throughout the picture. If the top right of a face is lit up on a subject matter, then the bottom left should be darker. The other areas should follow suit, with the top right being brighter and casting a darker shadow on the rest of the image. It sometimes helps to start with the base colors and then 'project' a shadow where no light would reach. While it sounds like an easy rule, beginners can easily find themselves forgetting. The result is an incongruous tattoo that might look nice, but could have looked better. You should also keep color theory in mind: using a complementary color like purple when shading green works better than using just gray. This is because the mind is tricked into thinking the complementary color is gray, while the color retains its vivid hue. It can make a tattoo pop nicely, so it's something to keep in mind!

Techniques And Technology

Of course, there are many ways to control shading with your machine. Some artists find that a higher speed makes shading much more smooth, and a higher amount of coils helps with this. Some artists even choose to use a shader bar rather than a shading pen to create solid transitions in large tattoos. Of course, this is all up to personal preference, and the advantages of machines can always be emulated by handiwork through hard work and practice.

Practice Is Key

If you want to improve your technique, the best way to do it is by practicing using a brush and water colors. Since you are naturally using the same inks to stain skin, the same techniques apply! However, paper is easier to practice on than skin. Finding a paper and ink that emulates your process correctly could take a while, and is different for every artists, since different artists use different inks and machines. But the end result will always be fantastic-looking shadows on your clients!

Tattoo inks

Tattoo inks consist of <u>pigments</u> combined with a carrier, and are used in <u>tattooing</u>.

Tattoo inks are available in a range of colors that can be thinned or mixed together to produce other colors and shades. Most professional <u>tattoo artists</u> purchase inks pre-made (known as pre-dispersed inks), while some tattooers mix their own using a dry pigment and a carrier.[1]

Tattoo ink is generally permanent. Tattoo removal is difficult, painful, and the degree of success depends on the materials used. Recently developed inks claim to be comparatively easy to remove. Unsubstantiated claims have been made that some inks fade over time, yielding a "semi-permanent tattoo."

Ink Type

Old school tattoo artists tend to have a sweet tooth for stable pigment-based inks, whereas new school artists tend to have a penchant for pre-dispersed inks. Before you get into specifics like price and color variety, you have to know which brands offer the core *type* of ink you prefer.

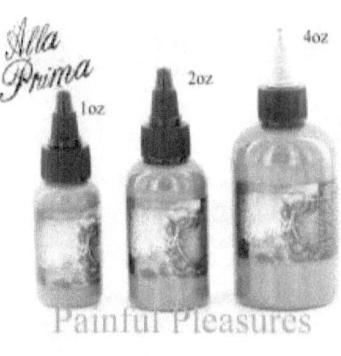

Alla Prima is *the* stable pigment-based ink available today, and quite literally the only one Painful Pleasures currently carries. All of our other inks are pre-dispersed and basically ready to use straight out of the bottle. You won't have to worry about mixing pigments (it really isn't advised with most pre-dispersed inks anyway), and they'll all have good flow that doesn't necessitate the thinning and extra mixing that stable pigments require.

Country of Manufacture & Presiding Regulations

11 of the top 14 tattoo ink brands Painful Pleasures carries are made in the U.S.A. Those brands include **Alla**

Prima Ink, Arcane, Bloodline (formerly Skin Candy), Dynamic, Eternal Ink, Fantasia, Formula 51, Intenze Tattoo Inks, Mom's Ink by Millennium Colors, Inc., Radiant, and Starbrite Colors Tattoo Ink. The 3 made internationally include **Kuro Sumi tattoo inks**, which are made in Japan, and Italian brands **Panthera Black Ink** and **Sacred Colors**. The Italian tattoo inks have to meet the doubly-strict standards of both the Italian Ministry of Health and ResAP 2008, which unifies much of Europe in an effort to protect consumers by regulating cosmetics, pesticides and pharmaceuticals more rigidly.

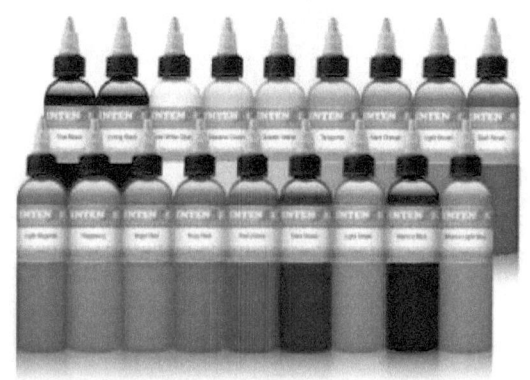

As tattoos have grown in popularity over the past few decades, the global tattoo community has made strides to deliver a continuously safer, more client-centric tattooing process. Manufacturers to distributors to shop owners and individual tattoo artists are more conscious than ever about sterility and safety in general. In that vein, conscientious tattoo ink brands have eliminated known carcinogens from their recipes. Not all ink is created equal, though; there are plenty of fraudsters manufacturing fake brand name inks and some legitimate ones that still use more chemicals than your clients may be comfortable with having injected into their skin.

Until regulations are in harmony with each other on an international level, the best thing you can do for your clients is purchase non-toxic inks made by brands that produce solvent- and PET plastic-free inks created using organic pigments. Some of your clients may only allow you to tattoo them with vegan-friendly tattoo inks made by brands with even stricter guidelines. (Note that there are still toxins found in nature, like heavy metals, so be cognizant of potential issues even with tattoo inks labeled organic.)

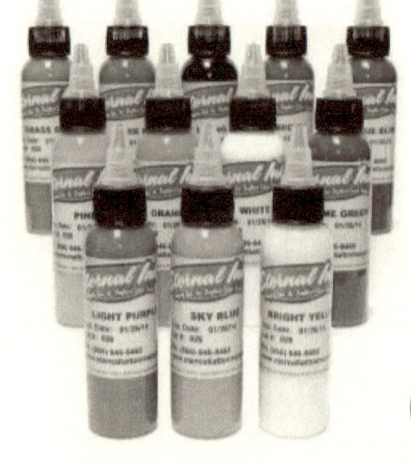

Organic & Vegan Tattoo Inks

A new wave of non-toxic tattoo inks made from organic pigments has emerged in recent years, after certain chemicals previously used in many tattoo inks started being linked to cancer. Brands like **Intenze**, **Eternal Ink**, **Formula 51**, and **Kuro Sumi** are at the forefront, saying that their pigments are all made from ingredients plucked straight from nature.

Eternal, Intenze, and Kuro Sumi take things a step further and tout that their inks are also vegan-friendly, because they do not include glycerin carriers derived from animal fat, pigments made from crushed bone, or any other animal products or bi-products.

Tattoo Ink Color Options

Variety is the spice of life, so it's no surprise that color selection can make a tattoo ink brand 3-pepper spicy or flat-out bland, depending how much diversity there is in the palette it covers. Brands like **Panthera Ink** have it rough, since their specialty is black inks… and there are only so many shades of black you can make en masse and sell successfully. (Panthera does offer a **Polar White Tattoo Ink** in addition to its 4 main black shades, by the way.)

Fortunately, black is the most-used "color", so a company specializing in black can still do a lot of business.

Out of all of the top tattoo ink brands, Painful Pleasures carries more **Intenze** and **Eternal Ink** options than it does for any other brand, so you'll have the greatest selection of colors, the most diverse kit choices, and the widest range of bottle size options per color if you shop these brands. However, if you're looking for some crazy color options, **Bloodline (Skin Candy)** and **Formula 51** are brands whose color catalogs you'll definitely want to scope out. Formula 51's catalog may only be 1/3 the size of Bloodline's presently, but how can you walk away without taking a closer look at pop

culture-inspired inks with names like
Clockwork
Orange, Crack Rock, Planet of the Grapes, and Smurfis Dermis?

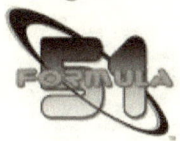

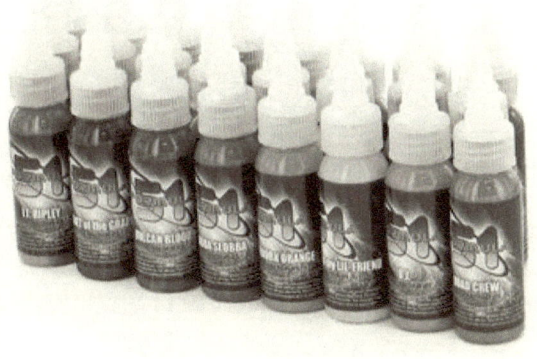

If you have the mentality that an individual brand's color palette doesn't really matter—that you can just pick and choose the colors you like best from each—you're only *partially* right. If you're a new school artist who prefers pre-dispersed ink, you may be disappointed to find that you can't always mix pre-dispersed inks very easily, particularly from different brands that utilize different carriers. If you want to mix colors to create your own unique shades, you should really try **Alla Prima's stable pigment-based inks**. If you're simply considering using different brands' colors *alongside* each other, you'll be able to do that more successfully. However, keep in mind that your clients may react to different brands and even colors within a brand differently; if you mix things up too much, you may not be able to easily tell them which ink caused a problem if they have a reaction. Additionally, different brands may yield different healing times. To keep things consistent and simple, and to achieve the best possible outcome for your client, it's ideal to stick to one brand.

To see our full selection of tattoo ink brands and the colors within each line, visit our **Tattoo Inks section**.

Tattoo Ink Prices

The best way to compare tattoo ink brand price differences is to look at what each brand normally charges for a 1 oz. bottle of tattoo ink (excluding sale prices), since not all brands carry other sizes like 0.5 oz., 2 oz., and 4 oz.

- Intenze and Sacred Colors are at the high end of the spectrum, with prices close to $10/bottle (at Wholesale prices)—Intenze because it's a truly premium brand, and Sacred Colors

because it's a high-quality imported brand.
- Bloodline/Skin Candy, Formula 51, Mom's Millennium Ink, Alla Prima Ink, Eternal Ink, and Arcane Ink are all in the $8.39-$8.75 range (listed from lowest to highest).
- Radiant, Dynamic, Fantasia, and Starbrite range from $7.00-$7.99 respectively.
- Kuro Sumi is available for $4.99 per 1 oz. bottle.

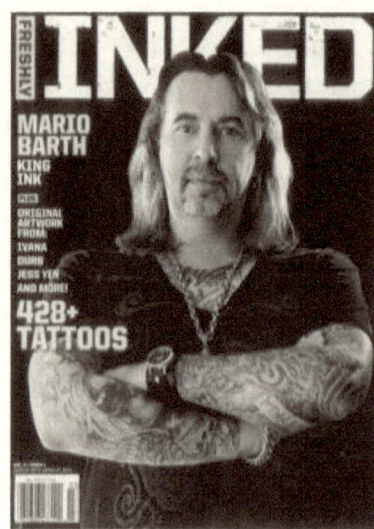

Innovation

At the end of the day, one of the most important factors to look at when comparing tattoo ink brands is who's taking the lead and paving the way for the tattoo industry. While every brand has its own unique angle and strives to meet its target clients' needs at the best price for the quality offered, there's one company that stands heads and shoulders above the rest in regard to company culture, quality, options, and innovation: **Intenze**.

Founded by world-renowned tattoo artist Mario Barth, Intenze has been setting the precedent for other tattoo ink brands for more than two decades. Intenze was the first ink brand to place value on sterilization, which drove up their costs at a time when no other company was spending money so "frivolously". Intenze has a unique approach to developing the inks it manufactures, too. It draws upon the experiences and needs of some of the world's best tattoo artists, who represent a wide range of styles, for help designing the colors and ink qualities that other similar artists will appreciate most!!

Top 5 Tattoo Ink Brands Made in the U.S.

With all of the different equipment required for tattooing, only one part of it actually stays around forever – the ink. Tattoo ink lives with people, under their skin. It becomes part of who they are.

Ink has come a long way from the days of sailor tattoos. Today there are almost too many options, and the cold, hard truth is many of those options are just not great. In order for a tattoo to live up to its potential, in terms of longevity and vivid color, the brand of ink has got to be of a high quality.

Tattoo professionals should research the different types of inks available, this will allow them to find the best fit for their art style.

These five top tattoo ink brands are made in the United States and are all of the highest quality. Read on to discover what sets each of them apart from the rest.

1. Eternal Ink

Eternal Ink is one of the oldest brands in the business. It was established in 1980 by Terry "Tramp" Welker. These water based inks are glycerol free, suitable for vegans and non-toxic.

The sheer variety of Eternal Ink is hard to match, with new colors constantly being introduced. Though the brand has been around for a very long time, it stays fresh by offering new varieties and **edging in on the hottest trends in ink** like flesh colors and white ink. The dark colors offered by Eternal Ink are among the best in the business, for both their vivid appearance and longevity.

2. **Intenze**

Intenze Tattoo Ink's mission is to work with tattoo artists to develop innovation. This U.S. company partners with artists to promote creativity in the industry and then translates that into the ink that's necessary to fuel the fire. With more colors available than any other brand on the market, Intenze allows artists the **fullest range of possibilities**. The colors are long lasting and the tattoo ink easy to work with in terms of flow and thickness.

Intenze prioritizes is safety. In order for an ink to be truly sterile, it has to be free of both mutagenic toxins and amines, and Intenze makes that happen with its ink. Every batch is verified sterile with a third party group to ensure the highest standards in safety. They're also vegan and compliant with both American and E.U. quality and safety requirements.

3. <u>Dynamic Inks</u>

There's no better word to describe Dynamic Ink: Intense.

In fact, the colors that come from Dynamic are so bright and focused that the company actually recommends using white to cut them, and using yellow to cut browns. These high-quality tattoo inks come in a wide variety of colors that allow artists to push their art to the next level.

These tattoo inks are made in the U.S. with premium pigments and are perfect for new school tattoo artists. The pre-dispersed pigment formula is easy to work with and feels great in the skin, going in easy and healing beautifully for long lasting quality. Designs stay true to color over time, maintaining that wonderfully intense color for clients.

4. Millennium Moms

Don't be fooled by the name; this isn't your mama's tattoo ink.

A pigment-based ink with feel and color that's hard to match, Millennium Moms Ink has been around since the mid-1990's and has been adopted by tattoo artists everywhere for its rich and innovative color line. Mom's Ink is top rated in terms of flow rate, pigment life and color consistency. It passes into the skin smoothly and beautifully, allowing artists to create designs that are eye-popping and full of movement.

What really sets Mom's Ink apart (aside from its high quality) is its line of Nuclear Colors **black light ink**, considered to be among the safest and brightest available. Mom's Ink took its expertise in pigment-based colors and brought it to black light.

5. Starbrite Tattoo Inks

If you're looking for staying power, then Starbrite is the brand for you. Created 25 years ago by Tommy Ringwalt, Jr., Starbrite Tattoo Inks offer an incredible variety of colors – a variety constantly expanding as Tommy travels the world consulting with artists to find out what they want to see. All Starbrite's tattoo ink is blasted with gamma radiation to kill all microorganisms. Developed in close connection with the FDA to follow strict guidelines, Starbrite is among the most rigorously tested and safest tattoo ink brands on the market.

This ink works well with a wide variety of tattoo styles, and is used by a wide range of tattoo artists to create their masterpieces. It's pigment-based, which gives it vivid color. The colors are pre-dispersed for ease of use. Tattoos completed with Starbrite are known to heal well and stay true to color over time.

This brand is built on quality and loyalty, and many artists use Starbrite exclusively. It's important to note that this brand is so popular it's widely imitated--so be sure to verify that you're buying authentic Starbrite ink from a professional source.

Tattoo ink is the medium through which a tattoo artist creates the beautiful, meaningful and fun designs that clients walk through the door for. High quality tattoo ink lasts longer, looks better, and feels better – that's why it's so important for tattoo artists to use the best for their clients.

Differences Between Rotary and Coil Tattoo Machines

If you're new to the Tattoo world, you may not yet be acquainted with the different types of machines available. But don't stress! We are here to help you with a breakdown of the most popular machine types and what makes each one special and unique.

At this moment you might not know the difference between rotary and coil tattoo machines, and if that's the case then you'll definitely want to read on. These differences matter for tattoo artists and for the clients who rely on them for the best quality tattoos possible.

Tattoo machines have developed from the days of crude, non-mechanical devices that poked the skin using human power to slick, complex pieces of technology that allow tattoo artists to create extraordinarily intricate designs that defy the imagination.

Understanding the qualities of tattoo machines will allow you to get more out of your tattoo artistry.

Types of tattoo machines

Before we dig in, it's important to note that these aren't the only types of tattoo machines. There are always new designs and models coming out that serve more specific functions. There are also other methods of tattooing that don't involve machinery.

Rotary and coil tattoo machines are the most popular and widely used. It's important to note that these machines don't live in isolation. You'll find that tattoo artists are constant innovators, and so there are always pieces being taken from one kind of machine and used on another as tattoo artists look to constantly make their machines better.

The basics are still the basics though, so even as there are tattoo artists who mix and match things up in terms of machines, the basic function of the tattoo machine remain the same.

Rotary tattoo machines

Invented in 1978 by German **Manfred Kohrs**, rotary tattoo machines are the original tattoo machine technology. Using an electric motor to drive the needles, this technology changed the way that tattooing was done, ushering in a new age of detail and control.

- Lightweight
- Easy handling
- Less hand and finger cramping
- Low noise output

- Single machine can be used for lining and shading
- Minimal adjustments needed
- Very popular among artists

Rotary machines move needles up and down using a small DC motor that's encased in a hard outer layer. These machines are of course incredibly simple, and they're still **widely used** throughout the tattoo industry.

Look for lots of innovations and add-ons to rotary machines that make them more efficient and even better than ever, as tattoo artists in the trenches constantly improving and adding their own spin to these stalwart machines.

- **Coil tattoo machines**

What's that buzzing noise? It's a coil tattoo machine!

The most common type of tattoo machine is the coil tattoo machine. The buzzing noise that's so readily associated with tattoo shops is the sound of the coil tattoo machine. It can be loud! That's not necessarily a bad thing, as it does allow the tattoo artists to focus just on what they're doing while drowning out all of the ambient noise.

Of course the coil tattoo machine isn't popular because of its decibel level, it's popular **because it works so well** and is so versatile.

There are three common types of coil machines; liners, shaders, and color packers. The name of these three types of coil tattoo machines pretty much sums up their intended use.

The liner runs a lot faster and not as deep as a shader or a color packer. The primary purpose of this type of machine is to create fine and precise line work, including the general outline of the tattoo.

Shaders are used to fill in color and primarily for shading in different gradients. These machines are set up to have a longer armature bar that hits significantly harder and deeper than liner machines. Shaders have a longer throw, allowing the shades to pack a little deeper into the skin.

Finally, the color packer tattoo machine is set up very similar to a shader because it is used to fill in color and blacks. This machine hits even harder and deeper than a shader, and does not work well for grey scale and shading gradients. It's best used to pack in colors solidly and more deeply than other machines. The purpose here is to "pack" in color and pigments with a single pass, rather than having to go over your work again.

Benefits of coil tattoo machines:

. Easy to regulate speed and power

- Easy to customize and interchange parts.
- Faster completion time
- Heavier weight allows a little more control
- Most popular type of tattoo machine

Coil machines generally come in **dual coiled form**, ranging from eight to ten wraps. The coils create the resistance that allows for that regulation we like with these machines, while an armature bar is pulled up and down quickly to inject ink into the skin.

Many tattoo artists swear by their rotary machines, believing them to be by far superior to anything else available. Coil machines offer immediate feedback to the artist when pressure is too much or too little. They tend to be used by newer tattoo artists who are wanting to have that more tactile and organic connection with the skin.

Choosing a tattoo machine for you

The best way to determine which tattoo machine is right for you is to try them out. If possible, **visit shops** or find vendors at trade shows that will allow you to test out these machines before you invest in one. You never know when you might suddenly find a tattoo machine that matches your art style perfectly.

Because the tattoo machine is **essentially the paintbrush** of this art form, getting the right one is an important step in the process of finding your way as an artist.

Whether you decide to go with a coil or rotary tattoo machine, look for high quality inks and accessories from Monster Steel to help you get the most for your clients.

NEVER BUY A CHEAP TATTOO KIT THEY WILL JUST HURT THE PEOPLE YOU A TATTOOING

THE INK IS NOT MADE WELL AND THE MACHINES ARE MADE LIKE

CRAP... SAVE YOUR MONEY AND BUY ALL GOOD QULITY STUFF

Below is information taken from the FDA's web site post on the issue. These kits are no good any any real artist will tell you this stuff is putting people at risk...

Recently, the Food and Drug Administration (FDA) became aware of a problem after testing inks in home use tattoo kits marketed by White and Blue Lion, Inc. FDA has confirmed bacterial contamination in unopened bottles of the company's inks.

According to Linda Katz, M.D., M.P.H., director of FDA's Office of Cosmetics and Colors, using these inks for tattoos could cause infection. "FDA has confirmed one case of skin infection involving a consumer that used this company's tattoo products," Katz says, "and we are aware of other reports linked to tattoo products with similar packaging."

According to Katz, "Tattooing poses a risk of infection to anyone, but the risk is particularly high for those with pre-existing heart or circulatory disease, diabetes or compromised immune systems."

She notes that injecting contaminated ink into the skin or using contaminated needles may result in infections at the site of the tattoo. Signs of localized infection include redness, swelling, weeping wounds, blemishes, or excessive pain at the site. If you experience any of these signs, seek medical care right away. Even after a localized infection has healed, the area may be permanently scarred.

Further, an infection that is left untreated or inadequately treated could spread through the bloodstream (a process known as sepsis). These infections may be associated with fever, shaking chills (rigors) and sweats. If these symptoms arise, treatment with antibiotics, hospitalization and/or surgery may be required.

White and Blue Lion, Inc. recalled contaminated products on July 11, 2014, but FDA is still concerned that consumers and professional tattoo artists may be purchasing or using contaminated home tattoo kits and inks from other distributors.

Specifically, how can you identify kits and inks that you should not use because they may be contaminated? FDA advises you to watch out for inks intended for permanent makeup or traditional body tattoos that:

- have no brand name, carry a dragon logo, and/or are missing the name and place of business of the manufacturer or distributor,
- are sold singly and in kits containing anywhere from five to 54, or perhaps more, bottles of inks of various colors, and
- are marked with "Lotch" [sic] and Batch numbers, and "Date produced" and "Best if used by" dates.

"If you're buying tattoo inks or getting a tattoo from a professional tattoo artist, you should first examine the products to determine whether the inks or kits meet the above descriptions," cautions Katz.

FDA's goal is to encourage consumers and tattoo and permanent make-up artists to take certain precautions and to urge potentially infected clients to seek medical care. "Reporting an infection to FDA and the artist is important in order for FDA to investigate, and to enable the artist to take steps to prevent others from becoming infected," says epidemiologist Katherine Hollinger, D.V.M., M.P.H., from the Office of Cosmetics and Colors.

Consumers and tattoo artists should do the following:

- Seek immediate medical care if you experience any signs of infection.
- Don't use tattoo inks and kits that have no brand name, carry a dragon logo, and/or are missing the name and place of business of the manufacturer or distributor.

- *Dispose of tattoo inks that meet this description.*
- *Do not use recalled kits.*
- *Report adverse events or side effects through FDA's* MedWatch Safety Information and Adverse Event Reporting Program.

How to Avoid a Tattoo Infection: Proper Aftercare

If you don't take care of your tattoo then you can risk infection, bubbling, ink fading, and bleeding – not something that anyone wants to encounter! Since tattoos open up the skin you must remember that your fresh ink is actually an open wound, and treat it accordingly. We've got the tips to show you how.

One of the most important aspects about getting a tattoo is learning how to take care of it properly in order to avoid the risk of a tattoo infection. While most tattoo artists will give you very detailed and specific instructions on the proper tattoo aftercare they want you to follow, many will also give you a head start by supplying you with a few ointment applications until you are able to get to the store for a more ample supply of your own. An essential aspect of this aftercare, however, is understanding the potential issues that you may face such as infection, rashes and skin keloids. Educating yourself on the "what ifs" could help you in more than enough ways. You will not only be able to identify an issue before it spirals out of control, but you will also be able to take the necessary precautions to avoid them starting altogether!

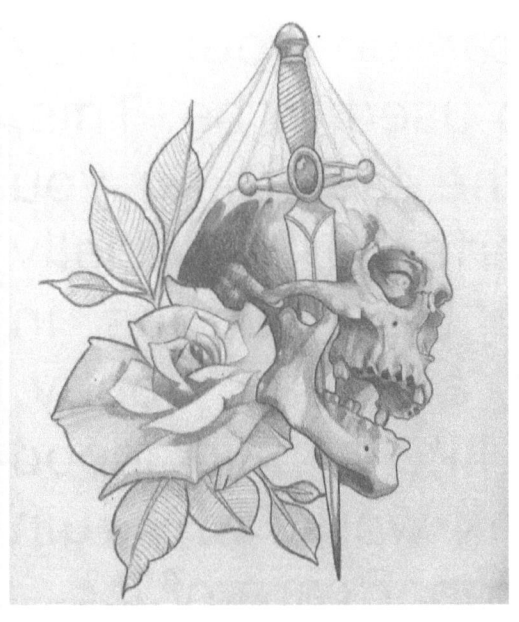

If you are able to quickly recognize a problem, you will be more likely to avoid a disfigured or discolored tattoo. Even when you get a tattoo infection, if handled and addressed immediately, you will be able to clear the infection and save the tattoo. As you will see from the following examples, if and when a tattoo infection does spiral out of control, chances are that you could be left with a scar on your body where your tattoo used to be. This, we are sure, is the last thing you will want to experience, especially due to the fact that tattoos in general, are not a cheap hobby. You more than likely paid good money for your ink work, why ruin it by not taking proper care of it?

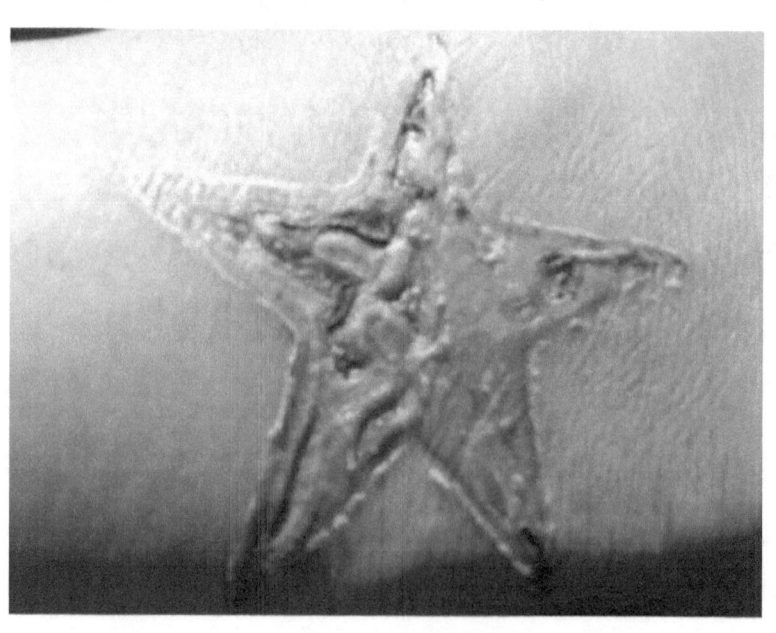

Keeping the area where you got your tattoo moisturized and clean at all times is vital to proper healing. While your skin adjusts to the ink, it will need moisture to help it settle and stretch properly. During the first few days, it is completely normal to experience raised skin in the area and shape of the tattoo – most people admit that it looks like the tattoo may have been branded on their skin. This is natural swelling caused by the ink in the under layers of the skin. During these first few days, the excess ink will push it's way out of the skin. You'll notice that as you apply ointment, the ink will seep onto your hands. Again, this is normal.

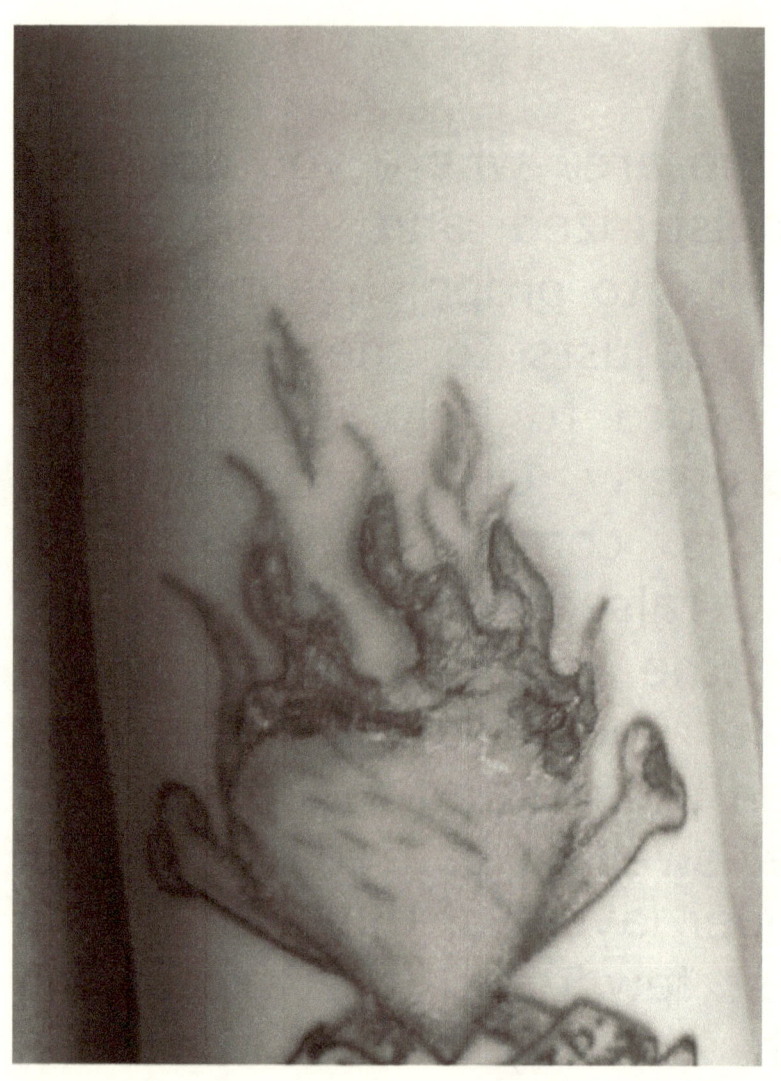

If you start to notice red bumps or rashes surrounding or on top of the tattoo, this may be signs that an infection is developing. You should advise your client call their tattoo artist immediately so they can determine if this is a reaction or an infection. Some reactions may look worse than they are. If you have sensitive skin, this may be a likely cause of irritation and does not necessarily mean that you have a tattoo infection.

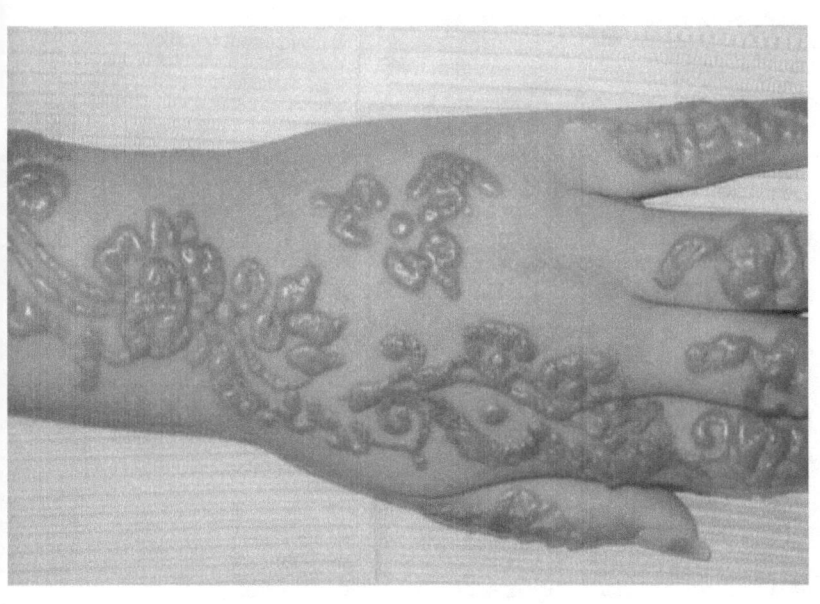

A tattoo infection can look many different ways depending on your skin or the severity of the infection. Many people experience skin keloids that quickly turn to a flaky, cracked lump on the skin. This can be on or around the tattoo area and if left unattended, it could actually grow to the point where the ink of the tattoo or no longer visible.

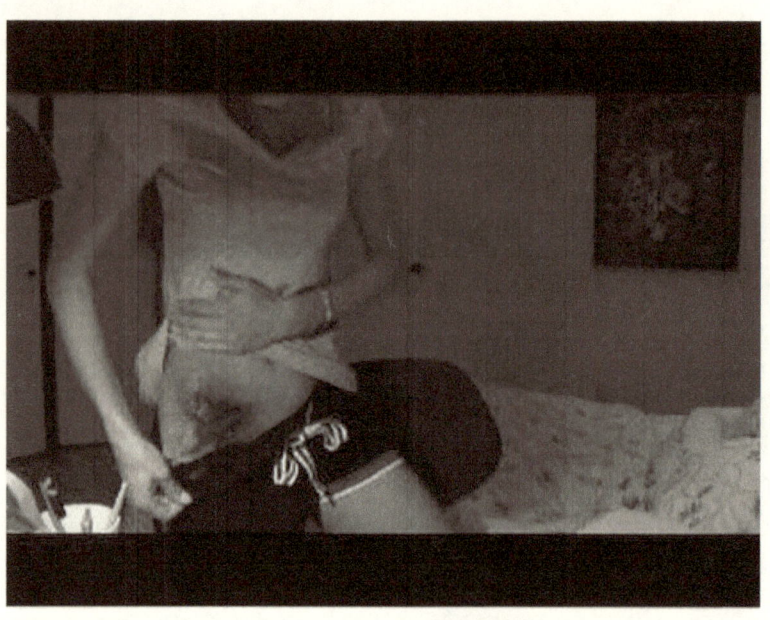

During the early stages of a tattoo infection, you may notice that the tattoo may become discolored. This is the first sign that something is wrong. While color ink may fade if proper aftercare is not followed such as washing with soap too soon or exposing the ink to the sun within the first 8 weeks, it should not discolor. Discoloration, in this regard means that green ink will turn to yellow ink or brownish in color.

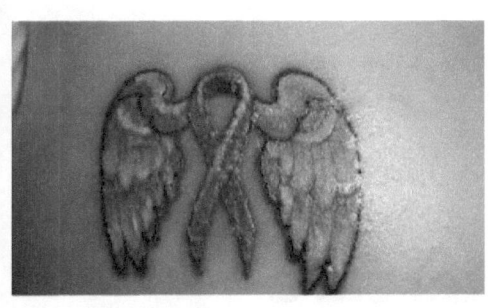

Another common form of a tattoo infection is when the skin surrounding the tattoo becomes coarse and brittle. You may feel the area tighten up and resemble a leathery like surface. This is a first sure-tell sign that the skin is not retaining moisture at all. When the skin is too dry, it can reject the ink and your body will attempt to fight off and contain what it thinks is a foreign object under the skin.

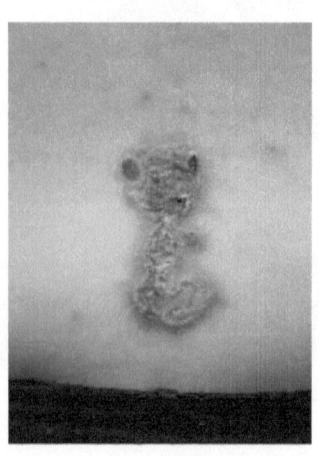

Proper Tattoo Aftercare

1. Only keep the tattoo covered for the first two hours after getting it done. Remove the bandage or wrapping after 1-2

hours to ensure that the ink has room to breath. The natural air will help the healing process begin

2. Keep the area clean and moisturized at all times. Use only the ointment that your tattoo artist recommends or a cream specifically for tattoo aftercare such as Tattoo Goo.
3. For the first few days, do not let water or soap directly touch the tattoo area. You can use a warm washcloth to go over the area and keep it clean
4. Avoid direct exposure to the sun, chlorine or salt water for at least 6-8 weeks

5. Do not use alcohol products on or around the area for at least 4 weeks
6. Do not pick the skin on the tattoo or rub abrasively
7. When applying ointment, rub in soft, circular motions until entire area is covered

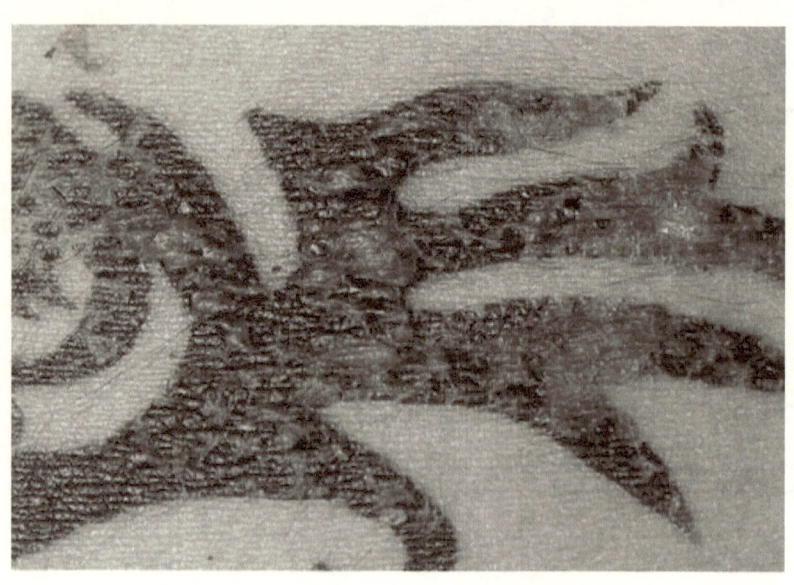

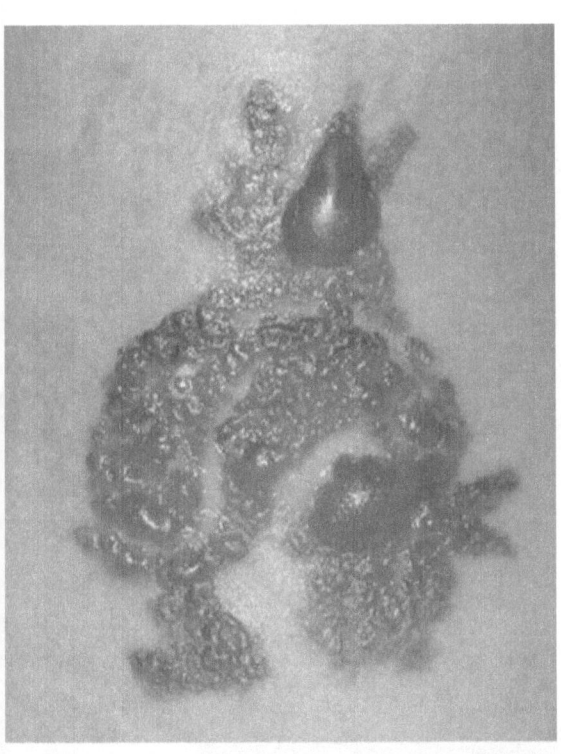
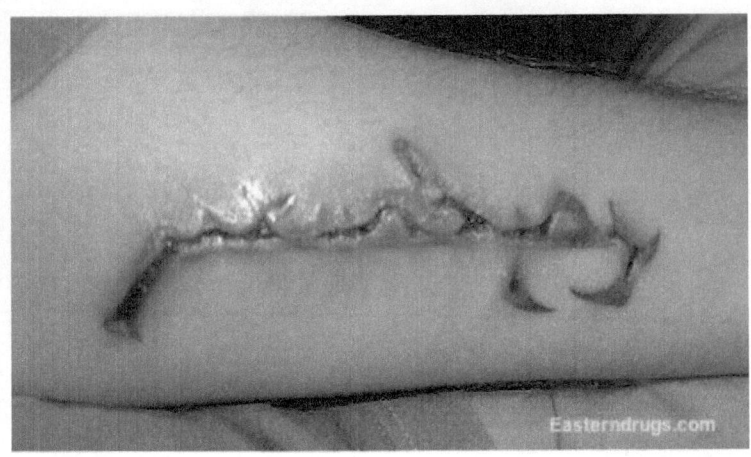

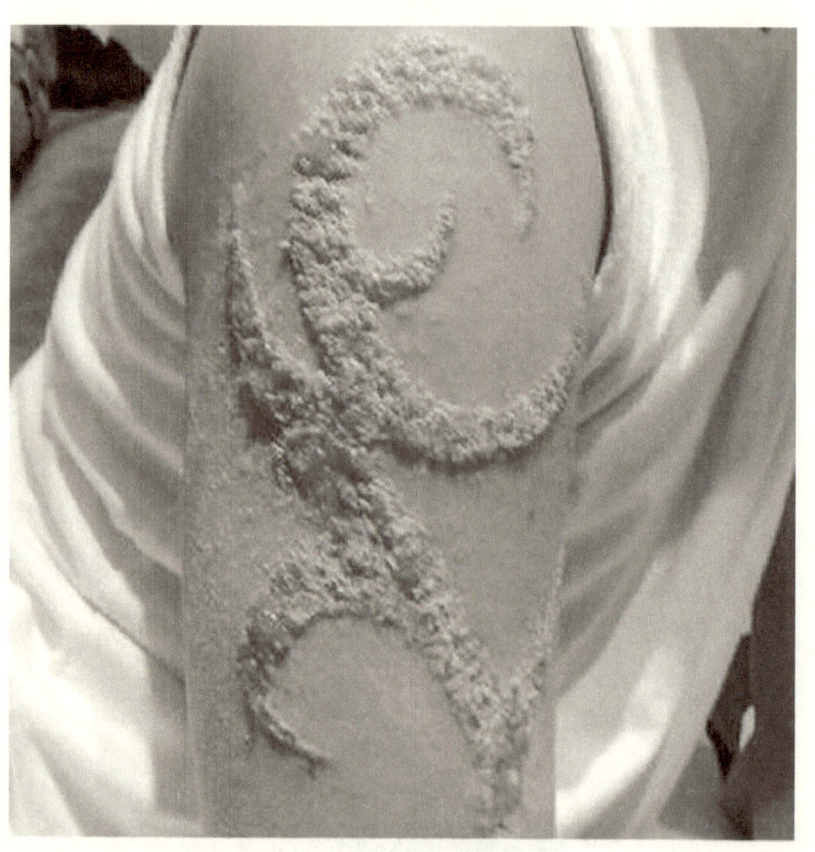

How to Make a Tattoo Stencil Out of Tracing Paper

⋮

By Jessica Reed

If you need to create the outline of a tattoo for someone, or just want to see what one would look like on you before you get it done, a tattoo stencil is the way to go. A tattoo stencil is way to transfer your tattoo design onto your skin to see what it will look like.

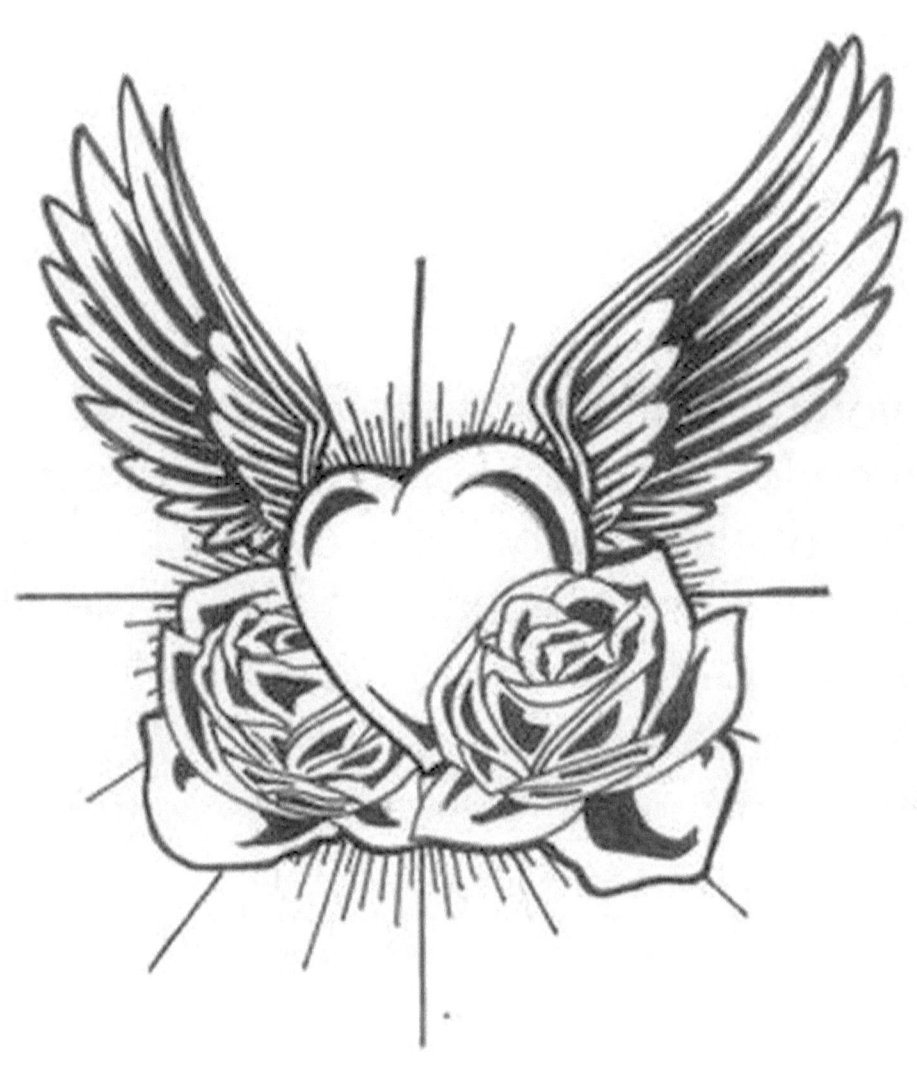

Step 1

Practice your tattoo design on a piece of paper. If you don't want to design your own, find a design online and print it off.

Step 2

Trace your tattoo design onto tracing paper using a technical pen with stencil ink. Make sure it is the right size for the area you want the tattoo. If not, redraw it to the proper size. Let the stencil dry completely.

Step 3

Clean the skin and wipe it dry. Press the tracing paper against the skin and hold it firmly. Remove it slowly and the tattoo should be outlined on the skin.

THIS IS ALL FOR NOW BROTHERS AND SISTERS!!!!

I hope you all enjoyed this book and if it was a big help well that's all I need to know. !!!

P.S

never ever tattoo in your home always seek help from a licensed professional if any person says they are a licensed artist and tattoos in there home RUN AWAY!!